CLASSICAL SOLOS
FOR
ALTO SAXOPHONE
VOLUME 2

T0083372

ONLINE MEDIA INCLUDED
Audio Recordings
Printable Piano Accompaniments

Speed • Pitch • Balance • Loop

To access recordings and PDF accompaniments, visit:
www.halleonard.com/mylibrary

Enter Code
4535-7304-8095-7072

ISBN 978-1-70516-752-6

Visit Hal Leonard Online at
www.halleonard.com

World headquarters, contact:
Hal Leonard
7777 West Bluemound Road
Milwaukee, WI 53213
Email: info@halleonard.com

In Europe, contact:
Hal Leonard Europe Limited
1 Red Place
London, W1K 6PL
Email: info@halleonardeurope.com

In Australia, contact:
Hal Leonard Australia Pty. Ltd.
4 Lentara Court
Cheltenham, Victoria, 3192 Australia
Email: info@halleonard.com.au

LARGO
from *Xerxes*

E♭ ALTO SAXOPHONE

GEORGE FRIDERIC HANDEL
Arranged by PHILIP SPARKE

Largo (♩ = 68)

Slower

SONGS MY MOTHER TAUGHT ME

from *Gypsy Songs*

ANTONÍN DVOŘÁK
Arranged by PHILIP SPARKE

E♭ ALTO SAXOPHONE

MINUET NO. 2
from *Notebook for Anna Magdalena Bach*

Eb ALTO SAXOPHONE

Attributed to CHRISTIAN PEZOLD
Arranged by PHILIP SPARKE

LA CINQUANTAINE
from *Two Pieces for Cello and Piano*

JEAN GABRIEL-MARIE
Arranged by PHILIP SPARKE

Eb ALTO SAXOPHONE

Moderato (♩ = 80)

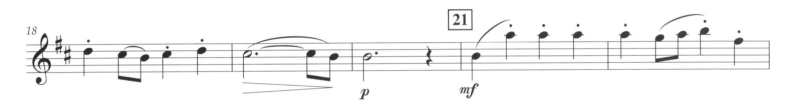

SEE, THE CONQUERING HERO COMES

from *Judas Maccabeus*

GEORGE FRIDERIC HANDEL
Arranged by PHILIP SPARKE

E♭ ALTO SAXOPHONE

SONATINA
Op. 36, No. 1

MUZIO CLEMENTI
Arranged by PHILIP SPARKE

Eb ALTO SAXOPHONE

00870105

SERENATA
from *String Quartet, Op. 3, No. 5*

E♭ ALTO SAXOPHONE

FRANZ JOSEPH HAYDN
Arranged by PHILIP SPARKE

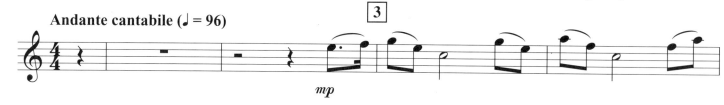

TAMBOURIN
from *Second Suite in E Minor*

JEAN-PHILIPPE RAMEAU
Arranged by PHILIP SPARKE

E♭ ALTO SAXOPHONE

WALTZ
from *Album for the Young*

PYOTR ILYICH TCHAIKOVSKY
Arranged by PHILIP SPARKE

E♭ ALTO SAXOPHONE

Vivace (♩. = 66)

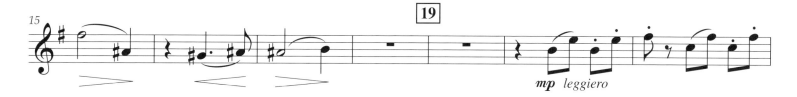

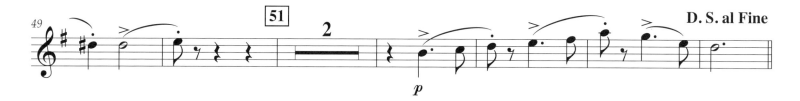

SONATINA
from *Six Pieces, Op. 3*

CARL MARIA VON WEBER
Arranged by PHILIP SPARKE

E♭ ALTO SAXOPHONE

GAVOTTE
from *Paride ed Elena*

Eb ALTO SAXOPHONE

CHRISTOPH GLUCK/arr. JOHANNES BRAHMS
Arranged by PHILIP SPARKE

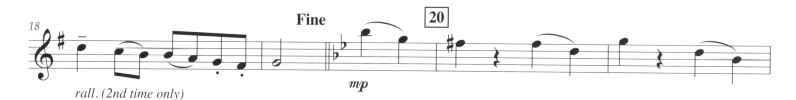

SONATA
Op. 118, No. 1

ROBERT SCHUMANN
Arranged by PHILIP SPARKE

Eb ALTO SAXOPHONE

00870105

SERENADE
from *Schwanengesang, D.957*

FRANZ SCHUBERT
Arranged by PHILIP SPARKE

E♭ ALTO SAXOPHONE

SONATINA
Anh. 5, No. 1

LUDWIG VAN BEETHOVEN
Arranged by PHILIP SPARKE

Eb ALTO SAXOPHONE

00870105

BOURRÉE
from *Flute Sonata, HWV 363b*

Eb ALTO SAXOPHONE

GEORGE FRIDERIC HANDEL
Arranged by PHILIP SPARKE

00870105